Power of Mental Imagery

by Warren Hilton

Copyright © 8/26/2015
Jefferson Publication

ISBN-13: 978-1517073541

Printed in the United States of America

Contents

Chapter I

IMAGINATION AND RECOGNITION

Recognizing the Past as Past

In the preceding volume of this *Course*, entitled "The Trained Memory," you learned that the memory process involves four elements, Retention, Recall, Recognition and Imagination; and the scope and operation of two of these elements, Retention and Recall, were explained to you.

There remain Recognition and Imagination, which we shall make the subject of this book. We shall treat of them, however, not only as parts of the memory process, but also as distinct operations, with an individual significance and value.

Both Recognition and Imagination have to do with mental images.

Recognition relates exclusively to those mental images that are the replica of former experiences. *It is the faculty of the mind by which we recognize remembered experiences as a part of our own past.* If it were not for this sense of familiarity and of ownership and of the past tense of recalled mental images, there would be no way for us to distinguish the sense-perceptions of the past from those of the present.

Recognition is therefore an element of vital necessity to every act of memory.

Imagination, Past, Present and Future

Imagination relates either to the past, the present or the future. On the one hand, it is the outright re-imagery in the mind's eye of past experiences. On the other hand, it is the creation of new and original mental images or visions by the recombination of old experiential elements.

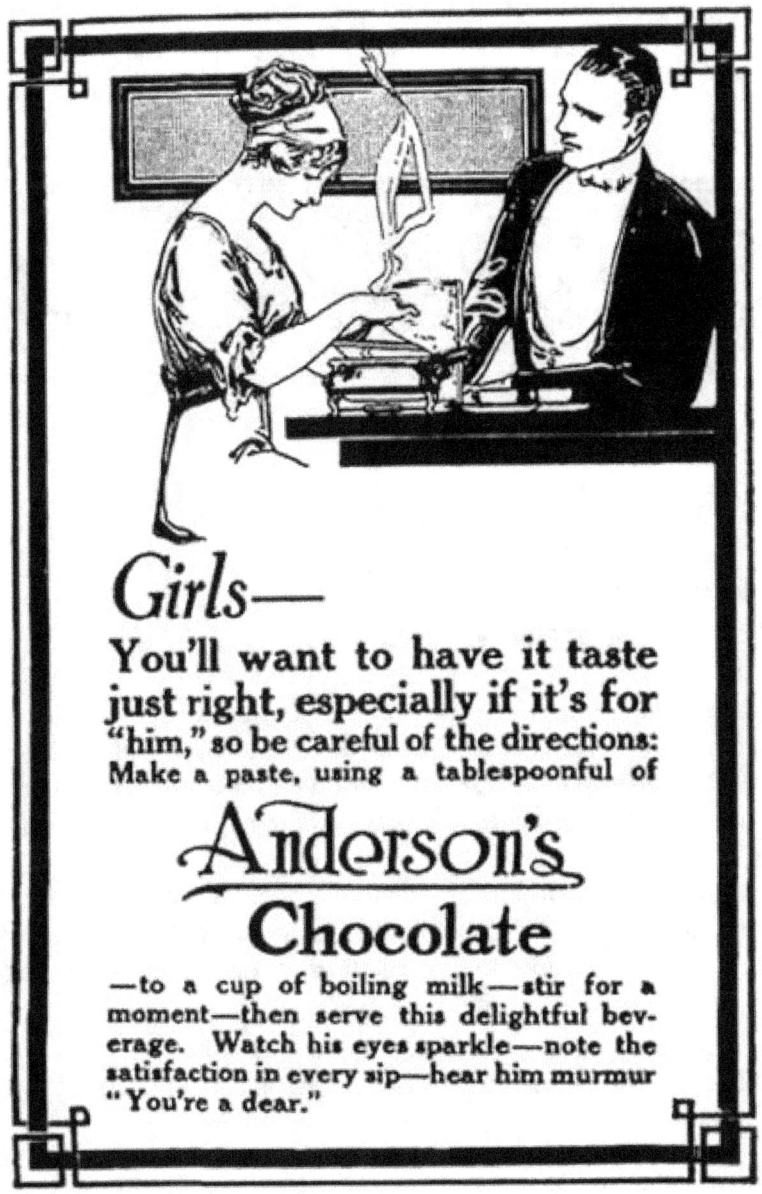

Girls—

You'll want to have it taste just right, especially if it's for "him," so be careful of the directions: Make a paste, using a tablespoonful of

Anderson's Chocolate

—to a cup of boiling milk—stir for a moment—then serve this delightful beverage. Watch his eyes sparkle—note the satisfaction in every sip—hear him murmur "You're a dear."

THIS ADVERTISEMENT COMBINES DIFFERENT ELEMENTS IN A SKILFUL APPEAL TO THE SENSES. SEE TEXT, PAGE 34
[Textual representation of advertisement]

KINDS OF MENTAL IMAGES

Chapter II

KINDS OF MENTAL IMAGES

Visual Imagery

When we speak of "images" in connection with Imagination and Recognition we do not refer merely to mental pictures of things seen. *Mental images are representations of past mental experiences of any and every kind.* They include past sensations of sound, taste, smell, feeling, pain, motion and the other senses, as well as sensations of sight. One may have a mental image of the voice of a friend, of the perfume of a flower, just as he may have mental images of their appearance to the eye. Indeed, the term "image" is perhaps unfortunately used in this way, since it must be made to include not only mental pictures in a visual sense, but all forms of reproductive mental activity.

Our recollection of past experiences may be either full and distinct or hazy and inadequate. Some persons are entirely unable to reproduce certain kinds of sensory experiences. Somehow they are aware of having had these experiences, but they cannot reproduce them. Every one of us has his own peculiarities.

Auditory Imagery

This morning I called upon a friend in his office. I was there but a short time. Yet I can easily call to mind every detail of the surroundings. I can see the exterior of the building, its form, size, color, window-boxes with flowers, red tile roof, formal gardens in the open court, and even many of the neighboring buildings. I can plainly recall the color of the carpet on his office floor, the general tone of the paper on the wall, the size, type and material of his desk, and many other elements going to make up an almost perfect mental duplicate of the scene itself. I can even see my friend sitting at his desk, and can distinctly remember the color, cut and texture of his clothing and just how he looked when he smiled.

Imagery of Taste and Smell

Last evening we entertained a number of friends at dinner. One of the ladies was an accomplished musician, and later in the evening she delighted us with her exquisite playing upon the piano. The airs she played were familiar to me. I am fond of music and I enjoyed her playing. I can sit here today and in imagination I can see her seated before the piano and remember just how her hands looked as she fingered the keys. But I find it difficult to recall the air of the selection or the tones of the piano. My mental images of the notes as they came from the piano are faint and uncertain and not nearly so distinct and clear as my recollection of the scene.

Muscular and Tactual Imagery

I find it easy to recall the appearance of the food that was served me for breakfast this morning. I can also faintly imagine the odor and taste of the coffee and toast, but I find that these images of taste and smell are not nearly so realistic as my mental images of what I saw and heard during the course of the meal.

When I was in college I was very fond of handball and was a member of the handball team. It has been many years since I played the game, yet I can distinctly feel the peculiar tension of the right arm and shoulder muscles that accompanied the "service." Nor do I feel the slightest difficulty in evoking a distinct mental image of the prickly sensations that so annoyed me as a boy when I would first put on woolen underwear in the fall of the year.

Personal Differences in Mental Imagery

From these examples, it is apparent that we can form mental images of past sensations of sight, sound, taste, smell and feeling, and indeed of every kind, including the muscular or motor sense and the sense of heat and cold.

But there is the greatest possible difference in individuals in this respect. Some persons have distinct images of things they have seen, are good visualizers. Others are weak in this respect, but have clear auditory images. And so as to all the various kinds of sensory images.

This is a fact of comparatively recent discovery. The first proponent of the idea was Fechner, but no statistical work was done in this line until Galton entered the field, in 1880. In his "Inquiries into Human Faculties," he says:

Investigations of Doctor Galton

"To my astonishment, I found that the great majority of the men of science to whom I first applied protested that mental imagery was unknown to them, and they looked on me as fanciful and fantastic in supposing that the words 'mental imagery' really expressed what I believed everybody supposed them to mean. They had no more notion of its true nature than a color-blind man, who has not discerned his defect, has of the nature of color. They had a mental deficiency of which they were unaware and naturally enough supposed that those who affirmed they possessed it were romancing."

Investigations of Professor James

The investigations of Dr. Galton were continued by Professor James, of Harvard University. He collected from hundreds of persons descriptions of their own mental images. The following are extracts from two cases of distinctly different types. The one who is a good visualizer says:

"This morning's breakfast-table is both dim and bright; it is dim if I try to think of it with my eyes closed. All the objects are clear at once, yet when I confine my attention to any one object it becomes far more distinct. I have more power to recall color than any other one thing; if, for example, I were to recall a plate decorated with flowers I could reproduce in a drawing the exact tone, etc. The color of anything that was on the table is perfectly vivid. There is very little limitation to the extent of my images; I can see all four sides of a room; I can see all four sides of two, three, four, even more rooms with such distinctness that if you should ask me what was in any particular place in any one, or ask me to count the chairs, etc., I could do it without the least hesitation. The more I learn by heart the more clearly do I see images of my pages. Even before I can recite the lines I see them so that I could give them very slowly word for word, but my mind is so occupied in looking at my printed image that I have no idea of what I am saying, of the sense of it, etc. When I first found myself doing this I used to think it was merely because I knew the lines imperfectly; but I have quite convinced myself that I really do see an image. The strongest proof that such is really the fact is, I think, the following:

"I can look down the mentally seen page and see the words that commence all the lines, and from any one of these words I can continue the line. I find this much easier to do if the words begin as in a straight line than if there are breaks. Example:

Etant fait
Tous ....
A des ....
Que fit ....
Ceres ....
Avec ....
Un fleur ....
Comme ....
(La Fontaine S. IV.)"

The poor visualizer says:

"My ability to form mental images seems, from what I have studied of other people's images, to be defective, and somewhat peculiar. The process by which I seem to remember any particular event is not by a series of distinct images, but a sort of panorama, the faintest impressions of which are perceptible through a thick fog—I cannot shut my eyes and get a distinct image of anyone, although I used to be able to a few years ago, and the faculty seems to have gradually slipped away. * * * In my most vivid dreams, where the events appear like the most real facts, I am often troubled with a dimness of sight which causes the images to appear indistinct. * * * To come to the question of the breakfast-table, there is nothing definite about it. Everything is vague. I cannot say what I see. I could not possibly count the chairs, but I happen to know that there are ten. I see nothing in detail. * * * The chief thing is a general impression that I cannot tell exactly what I do see. The coloring is about the same, as far as I can recall it, only very much washed out. Perhaps the only color I can see at all distinctly is that of the tablecloth, and I could probably see the color of the wall paper if I could remember what color it was."

This difference between individuals is just as marked in the matter of ability to form *auditory* images as in respect to *visual* images.

Investigations of Professor Scott

Thus, Professor Walter Dill Scott, of Northwestern University, cites the following:

"One student who has strong auditory imagery writes as follows: 'When I think of the breakfast-table I do not seem to have a clear visual image of it. I can see the length of it, the three chairs—though I can't tell the color or shape of these—the white cloth and something on it, but I can't see the pattern of the dishes or any of the food. I can very plainly hear the rattle of the dishes and of the silver and above this hear the conversation, also the other noises, such as a train which passes every morning while we are at breakfast. Again, in a football game I distinctly hear the noise, but do not see clearly anything or anybody. I hear the stillness when everyone is intent and then the loud cheering. Here I notice the differences of pitch and tone.'

"I had read that some people were unable to imagine sounds which they had heard, but it had not impressed me, for I had supposed that such persons were great exceptions. I was truly surprised when I found so many of my students writing papers similar to those from which extracts are here given: 'My mental imagery is visual, as I seem to see things and not hear, feel or smell them. The element of sound seems practically never to enter in. When I think of a breakfast-table or a football game I have a distinct image. I see colors, but hear no sound.'

A feature in the making of

Anderson's Cocoa

The manner in which thousands of pounds of Cocoa beans are daily roasted

Anderson & Co. N.Y.

THIS ADVERTISEMENT AWAKENS THE WRONG KIND OF MENTAL IMAGES. SEE TEXT, PAGE 34
[Textual representation of advertisement]

"Another in describing his image of a railroad-train, writes: 'I am not able to state whether I hear the train or not. I am inclined to think that it is a noiseless one. It is hard for me to conceive of the sound of a bell, for instance. I can see the bell move to and fro, and for an instant seem to hear the ding, dong; but it is gone before I can identify it. When I try to conceive of shouts I am like one groping in the dark. I cannot possibly retain the conception of a sound for any length of time.'

"Another, who seems to have no vivid images of any kind, writes: 'When I recall the breakfast-table I see it and the persons around it. The number of them is distinct, for there is only one of them on each side of the table. But they seem like mere objects in space. Only when I think of each separately do I clearly see them. As for the table, all I see is a general whiteness, interspersed with objects. I hear nothing at all, and indeed the whole thing is so indistinct it bewilders me when I think of it. My mental imagery is very vague and hazy, unless I have previously taken special notice of what I now have an image of. For instance, when I have an image of a certain person I cannot tell his particular characteristics unless my attention was formerly directed to them.'

"Another writes: 'There is no sound in connection with any image. In remembering, I call up an incident and gradually fill out the details. I can very seldom recall how anything sounds. One sound from the play "Robespierre," by Henry Irving, which I heard about two years ago and which I could recall some time afterward, I have been unable to recall this fall, though I have tried to do so. I can see the scene quite perfectly, the position of the actors and stage setting, even the action of a player who brought out the sound.'

"Quite a large proportion of persons find it impossible to imagine motion at all. As they think of a football game, all the players are standing stock-still; they are as they are represented in a photograph. They are in the act of running, but no motion is represented. Likewise, the banners and streamers are all motionless. They find it impossible to think of such a thing as motion. Others find that the motions are the most vivid part of their images. What they remember of a scene is principally movement.

"One writes: 'When the word "breakfast-table" was given out I saw our breakfast-table at home, especially the table and the white tablecloth. The cloth seemed to be the most distinct object. I can see each one in his place at the table. I can see no color except that of the tablecloth. The dishes are there, but are very indistinct. I cannot hear the rattle of the dishes or the voices very distinctly; the voices seem much louder than the dishes, but neither are very clear. I can feel the motions which I make during the breakfast hour. I feel myself come in, sit down and begin to eat. I can see the motions of those about me quite plainly. I believe the feeling of motion was the most distinct feeling I had. When the word "railroad-train" was given I saw the train very plainly just stopping in front of the depot. I saw the people getting on the train; these people were very indistinct. It is their motions rather than the people themselves which I see. I can feel myself getting on the train, finding a seat, and sitting down. I cannot hear the noise of the train, but can hear rather indistinctly the conductor calling the stations. I believe my mental imagery is more motile (of movement) than anything else. Although I can see some things quite plainly, I seem to feel the movements most distinctly.'

"A very few in describing their images of the breakfast-table made special mention of the taste of the food and of its odor. I have discovered no one whose prevailing imagery is for either taste or smell. With very many the image of touch is very vivid. They can imagine just how velvet feels, how a fly feels on one's nose, the discomfort of a tight shoe, and the pleasure of stroking a smooth marble surface."

HOW TO INFLUENCE OTHERS THROUGH MENTAL IMAGERY

Chapter III

HOW TO INFLUENCE OTHERS THROUGH MENTAL IMAGERY

A Rule for Influencing Others

The practical importance of the fact of mental imagery and of the individual differences in power of mental imagery is very great. They should be particularly taken into account in any business or profession in which one seeks to implant knowledge or conviction in the mind of another.

Application to Pedagogy

The underlying principle in such cases is this: *To the mind you are seeking to convince or educate, present your facts in as many different ways and as realistically as possible, so that there may be a variety of images, each serving as a clue to prompt the memory.*

We cannot do more at this point than indicate a few minor phases of the practical application of the principles of mental imagery.

In the old days geography was taught simply with a book and maps. Today children also use their hands in molding relief maps in sand or clay, and mountains and rivers have acquired a meaning they never had before.

In the days of the oral "spelling match" boys and girls were better spellers than products of a later school system, because they used not only the eye to see the printed word, the arm and hand to feel in writing it, but also the ear to hear it and the vocal muscles to utter it. And because of this fact oral spelling is being brought back to the schoolroom.

How to Sell Goods by Mental Imagery

If you have pianos to advertise, do not limit your advertisement to a beautiful picture of the mahogany case and general words telling the reader that it is "the best." Pianos are musical instruments, and the descriptive words should first of all call up delightful *auditory images* in your reader's mind.

If you have for sale an article of food, do not simply tell your customer how good it is. Let him see it, feel it, and particularly *taste it*, if you want him to call for it the next time he enters your store.

A Study of Advertisements

Turn, for example, to the advertisement of a certain brand of chocolate, facing page 6. The daintily spread table, the pretty girl, the steaming cup, the evident satisfaction of the man, who looks accustomed to good living,—these elements combine in a skilful appeal to the senses. Turn now to another advertisement of this same brand of chocolate, shown facing page 22. The purpose here is to inform you as to the large quantity of cocoa beans roasted in the company's furnaces. Whether this fact is of any consequence or not, the impression you get from the picture is of a wheelbarrow full of something that looks like coal being trundled by a dirty workman, while the shovel by the furnace door and the cocoa beans scattered about the floor remind one of a begrimed iron foundry.

The Words that Create Desire

The only words that will ever sell anything are graphic words, picturesque words, words that call up distinct and definite mental pictures of an attractive kind.

The more sensory images we have of any object the better we know it.

If you want to make a first impression lasting, make it vivid. It will then photograph itself upon the memory and arouse the curiosity.

A boy who is a poor visualizer will never make a good artist. A man who is a poor visualizer is out of place as a photographer or a picture salesman.

A Key for Selecting a Calling

No person with weak auditory images should follow music as a profession or attempt to sell phonographs or musical instruments or become a telephone or telegraph operator or stenographer.

No man who can but faintly imagine the taste of things should try to write advertisements for articles of food.

Remember the rule: *To the mind you are seeking to convince or educate present your facts in as many different ways and as realistically as possible, so that there may be a variety of images, each serving as a clue to prompt the memory.*

You can put this rule to practical use at once. Try it. You will be delighted with the result.

HOW TO TEST YOUR MENTAL IMAGERY

Chapter IV

HOW TO TEST YOUR MENTAL IMAGERY

Finding Out Your Weak Points

We suggest that you now test your own reproductive imagination with a view to determining your points of strength or weakness in this respect. And in doing so please bear in mind that the following questions are not asked with a view to determining what you know about the subject of the question, but simply how vividly—that is to say, with what life-like clearness—the mental image is presented to your mind, how close it comes to a present reality.

Tests for Visual Imagery

Go into a quiet room, close your eyes and try to bar from your mind every distraction. Now then, ask yourself these questions:

Visual.—1. Can you remember just how your bedroom looked when you left it this morning—the appearance of each separate article of furniture and decoration, the design and color of the carpet, the color of the walls, the arrangement of toilet articles upon the dresser, and so on? Can you see the whole room just as clearly as if you were in it at this moment? Or is your mental picture blurred and doubtful?

2. How clearly can you see the space that intervenes between your house and some far-distant object? Have you a clear impression of the visual elements that determine this distance?

3. Can you see a bird flying through the air? an automobile rushing down the street?

4. Can you imagine a red surface? a green surface? Try each primary color; which is most distinct to your mind's eye?

5. Can you see a smooth surface? a rough surface? a curved surface? a flat surface? a cube? Does the cube look solid?

6. When you memorize a poem do you remember just how each word looked on the printed page?

Tests for Auditory and Olfactory Imagery

Auditory.—1. Can you in imagination hear your door-bell ringing?

2. Can you form an auditory image of thunder? of waves breaking on a rocky shore? of a passing street-car?

3. Can you mentally hear the squeak of a mouse? the twitter of a bird? the breathing of a sleeping child?

4. Do these images come to you with the distinctness of reality?

5. Can you distinctly remember a voice you have not heard for a long time?

6. Can you recall the tones of an entire selection of music played on the piano?

Tests for Imagery of Taste and Touch

17

Smell.—Can you distinctly recall the odor of strong cheese? of violets? of roses? of coffee? of your favorite cigar? Is it clear to your mind that it is the odor you are recalling and not the taste?

Taste.—1. Can you remember just how butter tastes? an apple?

2. Try to imagine that you are sucking a lemon. Does it pucker your mouth? Does it seem like a real lemon?

3. Can you imagine the taste of sugar? of salt? of pepper?

Pain and Touch.—1. Can you in imagination live over again any past physical suffering?

2. Can you recall the feeling of woolen underwear? of bedclothes resting upon you?

3. Can you re-experience a feeling of exhaustion? of exhilaration?

Tests for Imagery of Heat and Cold

Heat and Cold.—Can you imagine a feeling of warmth? of cold? Does your recollection of the feeling of ice differ from your memory of a burn?

Go through the above list of questions, carefully noting down your answers. You will discover some personal peculiarities in yourself you never dreamed existed.

Try these questions on other members of your own family. You will be surprised at the varying results. You will perceive the reason for many innate differences of ability to do and to enjoy.

How to Cultivate Mental Imagery

Think what an immense part imagination plays in the world of business, and you will see how important it is to know your own type of sense-imagery.

To some extent the power of forming mental images can be cultivated so as to improve one's fitness for different kinds of employment. Such self-culture rests upon improvement in the vividness of your sense-perceptions. It suffices for your present purpose to know that to cultivate your power of sense-imagery in any respect you must (1) *Keep the appropriate sense-organs in good condition, and* (2) *When sense-perceptions of the kind in question come to you, give your undivided attention to your consciousness of them.*

THE
CREATIVE IMAGINATION

Chapter V

THE CREATIVE IMAGINATION

The Process of Creative Imagination

There is another type of imagination from the purely reproductive memory imagination of which we have been speaking in this book.

There is also Creative Imagination.

Creative Imagination is more than mere memory. It takes the elements of the past as reproduced by memory and rearranges them. It forms new combinations out of the material of the past. It forms new combinations of ideas, emotions and their accompanying impulses to muscular activity, the elements of mental "complexes." It recombines these elements into new and original mental pictures, the creations of the inventive mind.

Business and Financial Imagination

No particular profession or pursuit has a monopoly of creative imagination. It is not the exclusive property of the poet, the artist, the inventor, the philosopher. We tell you this because you have heard all your life of the poetic imagination, the artistic imagination, and so on, but it is rare indeed that you have heard mention of the business imagination.

The fact is no man can succeed in any pursuit unless he has a creative imagination. Without creative imagination the human race would still be living in caves. Without creative imagination there would be no ships, no engines, no automobiles, no corporations, no systems, no plans, no business. Nothing exists in all the world that had not a previous counterpart in the mind of him who designed it. And back of all is the creative mind of God.

How Wealth is Created

Mind is supreme. Mind shapes and controls matter. Every concrete thing in the world is the product of a thinking consciousness. The richly tinted canvas is the physical expression of the artist's dream. The great factory, with its whirling mechanisms and glowing furnaces, is the material manifestation of the promoter's financial imagination. The jeweled ornament, the book, the steamship, the office building, all are but concrete realizations of human thought molded out of formless matter.

Mind, finite and infinite, is eternally creative and creating in the organization of formless matter and material forces into concrete realities.

The Klamath Philosophy

Says Max Müller in his "Psychological Religion": "The Klamaths, one of the Red Indian tribes, believe in a Supreme God whom they call 'The Most Ancient One,' 'Our Old Father,' or 'The Old One on High.' He is believed to have created the world— that is, to have made plants, animals and man. But when asked how the Old Father created the world, the Klamath philosopher replies: *'By thinking and willing.'"*

How Men Get Things

We get what we desire because the things we desire are the things we think about. Love begets love. The man who is looking for trouble generally finds it. Despair is the forerunner of disaster, and fear brings failure, because despair and fear are the emotional elements attendant upon thoughts of defeat.

Behind every thing and every act is, and always has been, thought—thought of sufficient intensity to shape and fashion the physical event.

Mind, and mind alone, possesses the inscrutable power to create.

Your career is ordered by the thoughts you entertain. Mental pictures tend to accomplish their own realization. Therefore, be careful to hold only those thoughts that will build up rather than tear down the structure of your fortunes.

Prerequisites to Achievement

Creative imagination is an absolute prerequisite to material achievement.

The business man must scheme and plan and devise and foresee. He must create in imagination today the results that he is to achieve tomorrow. He must combine the elements of his past experiential complexes into a mental picture of future events as he would have them. Riches are but the material realization of a financial imagination. The wealth of the world is but the sum total of the contributions of the creative thoughts of the successful men of all ages.

How to Take Radical Steps in Business

With these principles before you, you can plainly see that the *creative imagination must be called upon in the solution of every practical question in every hour of the business day.*

Consider its part in two phases of your business life—first, when you are contemplating a radical change in your business situation; second, when you are seeking to improve some particular department of your business.

How to Take Radical Steps in Business

In the determination of how best you can better yourself, either in your present field of action or by the selection of a new one, take the following steps: (1) Pass in review before the mind's eye your present situation; (2) Your possible ways of betterment; (3) The various circumstances and individuals that will aid in this or that line of self-advancement; (4) The difficulties that may confront you. Having selected your field, (5) Consider various possible plans of action; (6) Have prevision of their working out; (7) Compare the ultimate results as you foresee them; (8) Decide upon the one most promising, and then with this plan as a foundation for further imaginings, (9) Once more call before you the elements that will contribute to success; (10) See the possible locations for your new place of business and choose among them; (11) Outline in detail the methods to be pursued in getting and handling business; (12) See the different kinds of employees and associates you will require, and select certain classes as best suited to your needs; (13) Foresee possible difficulties to be encountered and adjust your plans to meet them; and, most important of all, (14) Have a clear and persistent vision of yourself as a man of action, setting to work upon your plan at a fixed hour and carrying it to a successful issue within a given time.

The Expansion of Business Ideals

There is excellent practical psychology in the following from "Thoughts on Business":

"Men often think of a position as being just about so big and no bigger, when, as a matter of fact, a position is often what one makes it. A man was making about $1,500 a year out of a certain position and thought he was doing all that could be done to advance the business. The employer thought otherwise, and gave the place to another man who soon made the position worth $8,000 a year—at exactly the same commission.

Rising to the Emergency

"The difference was in the men—in other words, in what the two men thought about the work. One had a little conception of what the work should be, and the other had a big conception of it. One thought little thoughts, and the other thought big thoughts.

"The standards of two men may differ, not especially because one is naturally more capable than the other, but because one is familiar with big things and the other is not. The time was when the former worked in a smaller scope himself, but when he saw a wider view of what his work might be he rose to the occasion and became a bigger man. It is just as easy to think of a mountain as to think of a hill—when you turn your mind to contemplate it. The mind is like a rubber band—you can stretch it to fit almost anything, but it draws in to a small scope when you let go.

The Constructive Imagination

"Make it your business to know what is the best that might be in your line of work, and stretch your mind to conceive it, and then devise some way to attain it.

Little Tasks and Big Tasks

"Big things are only little things put together. I was greatly impressed with this fact one morning as I stood watching the workmen erecting the steel framework for a tall office building. A shrill whistle rang out as a signal, a man over at the engine pulled a lever, a chain from the derrick was lowered, and the whistle rang out again. A man stooped down and fastened the chain around the center of a steel beam, stepped back and blew the whistle once more. Again the lever was moved at the engine, and the steel beam soared into the air up to the sixteenth story, where it was made fast by little bolts.

"The entire structure, great as it was, towering far above all the neighboring buildings, was made up of pieces of steel and stone and wood, put together according to a plan. The plan was first imagined, then penciled, then carefully drawn, and then followed by the workmen. It was all a combination of little things.

Working Up a Department

"It is encouraging to think of this when you are confronted by a big task. Remember that it is only a group of little tasks, any of which you can easily do. It is ignorance of this fact that makes some men afraid to try."

Suppose, now, that instead of making a radical change in your business situation, you are simply seeking to improve some particular department of your business.

Imagination in Handling Employees

In commercial affairs men are the great means to money-making, and efficient personal service the great key to prosperity. In your dealings with employees do not be guided by the necessities of the moment. Expediency is the poorest of all excuses for action. Have regard not only for your own immediate needs, but also for the welfare and future conduct of your employees. It is part of the burden of the executive head that he must do the forethinking not only for himself but for those under him.

Perhaps the man you have under observation for advancement to some executive position has all the basic qualifications of judicial sense, discrimination and attentiveness to details, but you are uncertain whether he has enough imagination to devise new ways and means of doing things and developing business in new fields. If you wish to try a simple but very effective test along this line, you can adopt the following standard psychological experiment, which has been used at Harvard, Cornell and many other colleges and schools.

How to Test an Employee's Imagination

Let fall a drop of ink on each of several pieces of white paper, letterhead size. This will make irregular blotches of varying forms. Let the subject be seated at a desk and ask him to write briefly about what he sees in each blotched sheet, whether it be an animal form suggested by the outline of the blot, or anything else that comes into his mind while looking at the black spot. The principle involved here is the same as that involved in seeing pictures in a flickering log fire or having a vision of past or future events by gazing into a crystal. In any of these cases, it is not the blot, the fire or the crystal that produces the vision, but the creative imagination that recombines old elements into new forms. The number of images suggested to one by certain standard forms of ink-blot when compared with established results is a measure of his imaginative ability.

Imagination in Business Generally

In the choice of a location for your factory or store, you must foresee its future traffic and transportation possibilities. In passing upon a proposed advertisement you must get inside the head of the man on the street and see it as he will see it. In the purchase of your stock of goods you must gauge the trend of popular taste and foresee the big demand. In your dealings with creditors you must plan a course of action that will enable you to settle the account to *your* best interest at *their* request. You must find a way to collect from your debtors and at the same time hold their business. And so in a hundred thousand different ways you are constantly required to use creative thought in laying every stone in the structure of your fortune.

Imagination and Action

Do not understand us as saying that imagination, as the term is popularly used, is all you need. There must be also action, incessant, persistent. But *creative imagination, in a psychological and scientific sense, begets action. Every thought carries with it the impellent energy to effect its realization.* Use your imagination in your business and the action will take care of itself. Given imagination and action, and you are sure to win.